Walk Around

By Lou Drendel
Color by Don Greer
Illustrated by Ernesto Cumpian

P-47 Thunderbolt

Walk Around Number 11

squadron/signal publications

INTRODUCTION

Juggernaut n. 1. An overwhelming, advancing force that crushes or seems to crush everything in its path.

Though the manufacturer named it the Thunderbolt, it was more popularly known as the *Jug*, which may or may not have been short for *Juggernaut*. Whether or not this was simply a polite attempt to cultivate the less flattering sobriquet from which it is derived, **Juggernaut** is an apt description for one of the toughest and most successful fighters of World War II.

The P-47 was designed by Republic Aviation's chief engineer, Alexander Kartveli, whose P-43 Lancer was one of the more notable fighters of the 1930s. Republic had proposed a follow-on to the P-43, that was known as the P-44 "Rocket", and the U.S. Army Air Corps had responded with orders for more than 900 Rockets before the first example flew. Then, as now, there was a battle over fighter concept — small, nimble, lightweight, or big, heavy, and rugged. Kartveli was concentrating on the former until reports from Europe convinced him that a heavily armed, long-range fighter would be more successful in that war. The result was a complete overhaul of the P-44, which metamorphosed into the XP47A in it's lightweight Allison-engined version, and thence to the XP-47B with the Pratt & Whitney XR-2800 turbo-supercharged 2,000 hp engine which would give it a top speed of over 400 mph.

The promise of this performance was enough to win a $56 million contract for Republic to produce 773 Thunderbolts before the prototype had even flown! The XP-47B first flew on 6 May 1941, with test pilot Lowery L. Brabham at the controls. The first production Thunderbolt first flew in the fateful month of December 1941. Production Thunderbolts began to reach the Air Corps the following May; and before production was terminated 15,683 Thunderbolts would be delivered, making it the most-produced American fighter ever.

Comparisons to Axis or other Allied fighters were striking. It was more than twice as heavy as a Zero, ME-109 or Spitfire, and 50% heavier than the Fw-190 or P-51. P-47s were supplied to Great Britain, France, USSR, Brazil, and Mexico. The Thunderbolt was a world-wide participant in World War II, and fought on in many of the post war conflicts in the former colonies of many allied nations. It was one of the most successful fighters of World War II, from air-to-air to air-to-ground operations. It was able to survive punishing strafing missions after making a major contribution to clearing the European skies of some the best fighters ever built, and flown by the most experienced fighter pilots in the world at the time — the Luftwaffe. It was indeed, a *Juggernaut*.

Acknowledgements

Norm Taylor, my good friend and very consistent long-time contributor, dug deep into a very large database of prints and negatives to come up with vintage photos which greatly enhance the detail photographs of some fine restorations. I am indebted to the Lone Star Flight Museum, and the Kalamazoo Air Museum, aka "Air Zoo" for their permission to climb on their airplanes to shoot the detail pictures contained herein. Ted Adams, fellow T-34 partisan, and former WWII P-47 pilot, shared much of his Thunderbolt memorabilia.

(Overleaf) One of the truly outstanding Thunderbolt restorations is a recreation of the P-47 flown by Howard M. Park of the 513th squadron of the 406th Fighter Group. BIG ASS BIRD II was painstakingly restored by Blue Sky Aviation in Sellersburg, Indiana under the stewardship of Charles Osborn. Seen here at Oshkosh in 1995. (Lou Drendel)

ISBN 0-89747-

If you have any photographs of aircraft, armor, soldiers or ships of any nation, particularly wartime snapshots, why not share them with us and help make Squadron/Signal's books all the more interesting and complete in the future. Any photograph sent to us will be copied and the original returned. The donor will be fully credited for any photos used. Please send them to:

Squadron/Signal Publications, Inc.
1115 Crowley Drive
Carrollton, TX 75011-5010

Если у вас есть фотографии самолётов, вооружения, солдат или кораблей любой страны, особенно, снимки времён войны, поделитесь с нами и помогите сделать новые книги издательства Эскадрон/Сигнал ещё интереснее. Мы переснимем ваши фотографии и вернём оригиналы. Имена приславших снимки будут сопровождать все опубликованные фотографии. Пожалуйста, присылайте фотографии по адресу:

Squadron/Signal Publications, Inc.
1115 Crowley Drive
Carrollton, TX 75011-5010

軍用機、装甲車両、兵士、軍艦などの写真を所持しておられる方はいらっしゃいませんか？どの国のものでも結構です。作戦中に撮影されたものが特に良いのです。Squadron/Signal社の出版する刊行物において、このような写真は内容を一層充実し、興味深くすることができます。当方にお送り頂いた写真は、複写の後お返しいたします。出版物中に写真を使用した場合は、必ず提供者のお名前を明記させて頂きます。お写真は下記にご送付ください。

Squadron/Signal Publications, Inc.
1115 Crowley Drive
Carrollton, TX 75011-5010

(Front Cover) Colonel David C. Schilling climbs out of his P-47D. Schilling was a commander of the 56th Fighter Group and a 22.5 kill ace. The character on the nose of his Thunderbolt is "Hairless Joe", one of the many creations from the fertile mind of cartoonist Al Capp, creator of "lil' Abner".

(Back Cover) *Little Demon* was a P-47D flown by 18 kill ace Walter C. Beckham, commander of the 351st Fighter Squadron, 353rd Fighter Group.

The eleventh of 171 P-47Bs built carries extra cockpit glass at the rear of the canopy and short cowl flaps.The glass at the rear of the canopy was later removed. (Norm Taylor Collection)

The P-47B was redesignated RP-47B, the R standing for "Restricted" as a result of failure of the fabric covered tail surfaces, which caused flight restrictions to be enforced. Most were later recovered with metal surfaces. (Norm Taylor Collection)

A P-47D-6-RE Thunderbolt of the 78th Fighter Group. 350 of this version were built. (Norm Taylor Collection)

A fresh P-47D-22-RE is towed from the Republic factory. This model was the first to use the Hamilton Standard Hydromatic paddle blade propeller. (Norm Taylor Collection)

The authentic restoration of "Little Demon", the P-47 flown by Walter C. Beckham of the 351st Fighter Squadron, 353rd Fighter Group in late 1943 and early 1944 includes the USAAF data designation on the left side of the fuselage. (Lou Drendel)

The original "Little Demon" was a P-47D-5-RE, in which Beckham was shot down on 22 February 1944, becoming a P.O.W. At the time, he was the leading ace in the ETO with 18 victories. (Lou Drendel)

The modem day "Little Demon" was restored by Ray Stutsman, of Elkhart, Indiana, in the early 1980s. It was eventually sold to the Lone Star Flight Museum in Galveston, Texas, where it resides today as part of one of the most impressive collections of flyable World War II aircraft in the world. (Lou Drendel)

Though painted in an authentic matte finish for the restoration, however time and polish have modified the finish of "Little Demon" to gloss Olive Drab upper surfaces and gloss Neutral Gray lower surfaces. (Lou Drendel)

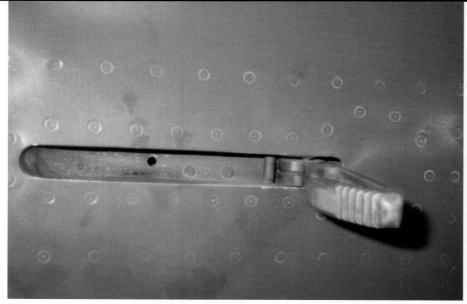

(Above) The retractable hand hold on the port side of the fuselage of the P-47 in the fully extended position. (Lou Drendel)

(Right) The kick-in step on the fuselage of the P-47 is a necessary aid to mounting the Thunderbolt. (Lou Drendel)

(Below) The retractable hand hold in use. (Lou Drendel)

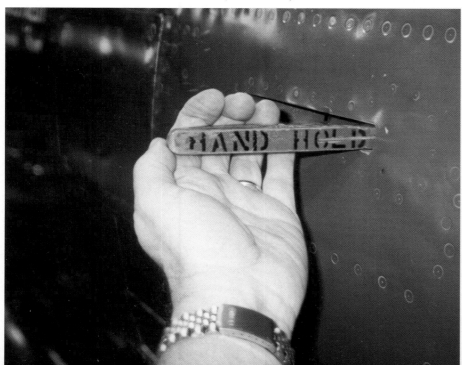

(Above) A P-47D-20-RE (43-25429) of the 19th Fighter Squadron, 318th Fighter Group, on Ie Shima in 1944. 300 of this model were built by Republic. (Norm Taylor Collection)

"Miss Mary Lou" on another day, another mission, this time with bombs. The Thunderbolt could carry a pair of 1,000 pound bombs on its wing stations. (Norm Taylor Collection)

"Vicky", the P-47D-6-RE flown by Earl Peterson of the 84th Fighter Squadron, 78th fighter Group at Duxford, England in 1944. (Norm Taylor Collection via G.L. Fry)

"Big Stud" the P47D-10-RE (42-75008) flown by Lt. Col. Bob Baseler, CO of the 325th Fighter Group. (Norm Taylor Collection)

The stainless steel turbosupercharger exhaust under the rear fuselage. (Lou Drendel)

Fuselage wing root louvers vent heat from the fuselage. (Lou Drendel)

(Above) Forward gunsight bead on top of the nose. (Lou Drendel)

(Above) Stencil on the lower starboard cowl flap. (Lou Drendel)

(Below) The exhaust vents on starboard side of nose. The forward vent is the oil cooler exhaust variable shutter, the middle vent is a fixed deflector, and the rear (round) is the excess exhaust gate. (Lou Drendel)

(Above) The exhaust manifold behind the open cowl flaps on the starboard side of the nose. (Lou Drendel)

(Left) Port side of "Little Demon's" cowling at the Lone Star flight Museum. (Lou Drendel)

(Below) The port side exhaust vents are a mirror image of the starboard exhaust vents. (Lou Drendel)

"WILDCAT" ("Nadine") was used often and hard at Bradley Field, Connecticut by the 121st CCTS-F in 1944. The result was that much of the OD paint job was eventually worn off. 42-74801 was a P-47D-6-RE. (Lt Col Mike Moffitt, USAF (ret) via Norm Taylor Collection)

(Above) A P-47D-23-RE of the Ist Air Commando Group at Barrackpore, India in March of 1945. The Air Commandos operated a wide range of aircraft in the China-Burma-India (CBI) theater in 1944 and 1945, supporting Wingate's Raiders. (Pete Bowers via Norm Taylor Collection)

(Below) A trio of Thunderbolts from the 121st CCTS-F, out of Bradley Field, Connecticut in 1944. (Lt Col Mike Moffitt, USAF (ret) via Norm Taylor Collection)

The rear fuselage of the Lone Star P-47, showing lower rudder hinge. The "bump" under the fuselage is a jack attachment point. Although this Thunderbolt is painted to represent the P-47D-5-RE flown by Walter Beckham, the small white placard identifies it as a Curtiss built P-47G-5-CU, with the incomplete serial number of "42-24-68". (Lou Drendel)

The small whip antenna (middle of white stripe) is for modern avionics. The rudder trim tab is chain-driven and adjustable by the pilot. (Lou Drendel)

The small, ground-adjustable trim tab on the elevator of the P-47 is meant to fine-tune the trim of the aircraft so that the cockpit-adjustable larger tabs are in the "0" position when the aircraft is in flight at cruise speed. (Lou Drendel)

Initial production P-47Bs had fabric covered elevators which had the fatal tendency to "balloon" and tear under the heavy aerodynamic loads of high speed flight. After at least two crashes were traced to this phenomenon, the elevators of P-47Bs were retrofitted with metal skins. All production aircraft after the B model had metal skins. The white bands on the vertical and horizontal tail surfaces, as well as the white band on the nose, was an identification feature of early P-47s, meant to distinguish the Thunderbolt from the Fw 190 for nervous allied anti-aircraft gunners. (Lou Drendel)

(Right) The elevator torque tube runs from just outboard of the trim tab, through the rudder cutout connecting the elevators. (Lou Drendel)

As rugged as they were, the stabilizers were not designed to support the weight of the rear fuselage, and any lifting of the aircraft had to be done using the lower jack point. (Lou Drendel)

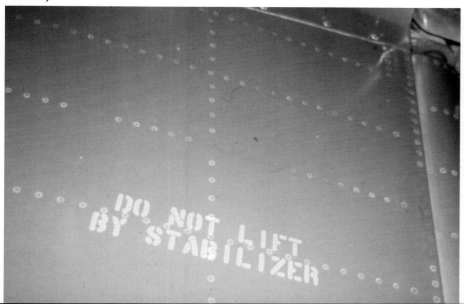

13

P-47 Development

P-35A

P-43

XP-47B

P-47B

P-47C-1-RE

P-47D-2-RE

P-47D-20-RE

P-47D-25-RE

P-47G-15-CU

P-47D-40-RA

P-47N-5-RE

XP-72

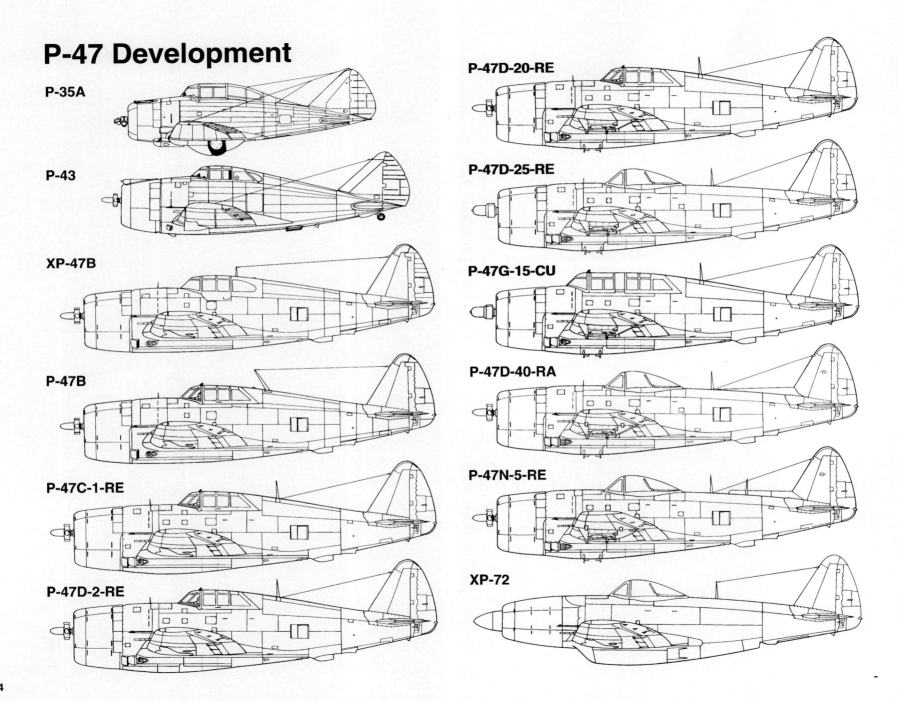

Main Assembly Components

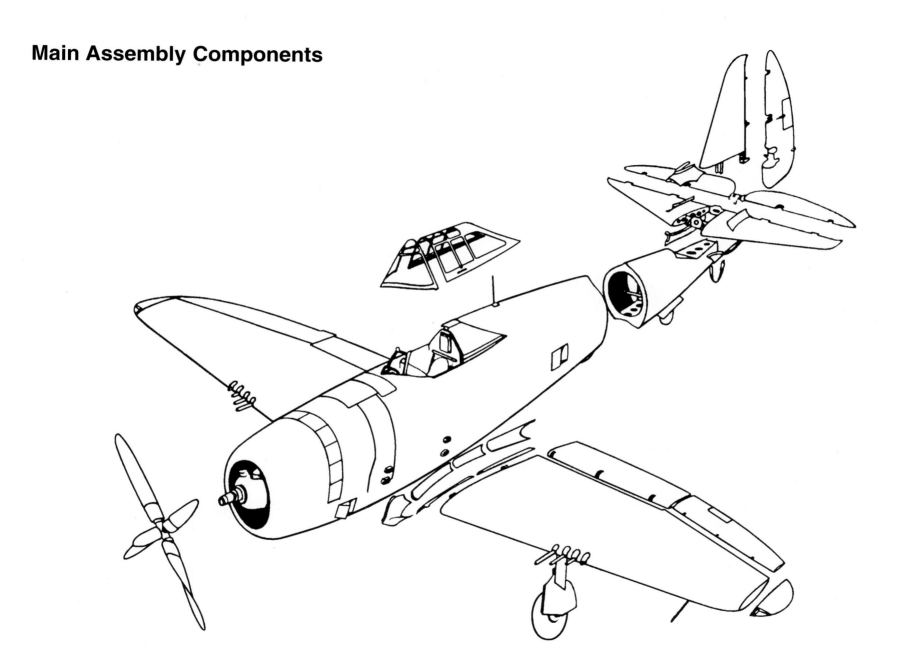

"Little Demon" made its first Oshkosh appearance in 1984, shortly after completion of
what was one of the most authentic restorations of the P-47 Thunderbolt. (Lou Drendel)

The elevator torque tube carried through a
rudder cut out connecting the right and left
elevators. (Lou Drendel)

The rudder trim tab worm and screw actuating mechanism is
covered by a small fairing on the left side of the rudder only.
(Lou Drendel)

Detail of the elevator hinge and cut out. (Lou Drendel)

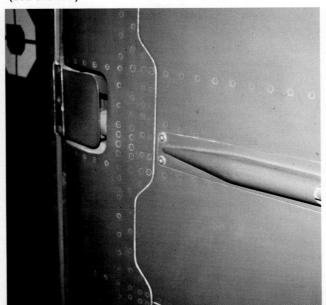

Fuselage Skin and Access Panels

(Above) "THE FLYING ABORTION" was a blue-striped P-47D-23-RA of the Ist Air Commando Group seen at Kiangwan Airdrome at Shanghai, China on 6 December 1945. It is in company with a B-25 and several Hump-flying C-46s. The immense space of the CBI, coupled with limited navigational aids led to the installation of Radio Direction Finding (DF) antennas behind the cockpit of P-47s. (Pete Bowers via Norm Taylor Collection)

(Left) A P-47C-2-RE (41-6298) in the foreground and a P-47C-5-RE at the rear of the 133rd CCTS-F out of Hillgrove Field, NJ in 1944. 556 "C" models were built by Republic. It was the first variant to incorporate all-metal tail surfaces in production and also featured a fuselage lengthened by eight inches (added forward of firewall) which improved flight characteristics. (Lt Col Mike Moffitt, USAF (ret) via Norm Taylor Collection)

(Below) A P-47D-23-RA of the Ist Air Commando Group in India during 1944. The relatively short range of the Thunderbolt on internal fuel required large external tanks for ferry missions over the Hump. Since all fuel had to be delivered by air to remote bases, the Thunderbolt saw limited service. It replaced P-51As with the group, but was in turn replaced in many units by the longer legged P-51D. (Norm Taylor Collection)

Armorers of the 318th Fighter Group range the guns of "Lady Ruth", a P-47D-I5-RE. The inboard guns are adjusted to have their bullet stream converge at 750 feet in front of the Thunderbolt. At that range, bullets from all eight .50 caliber machine guns will be within a 4-1/2 foot bulls-eye. At 600 rounds per minute, a one second burst would deliver 80 rounds to the target. This was more than enough firepower to bring down any enemy fighter. (Norm Taylor Collection)

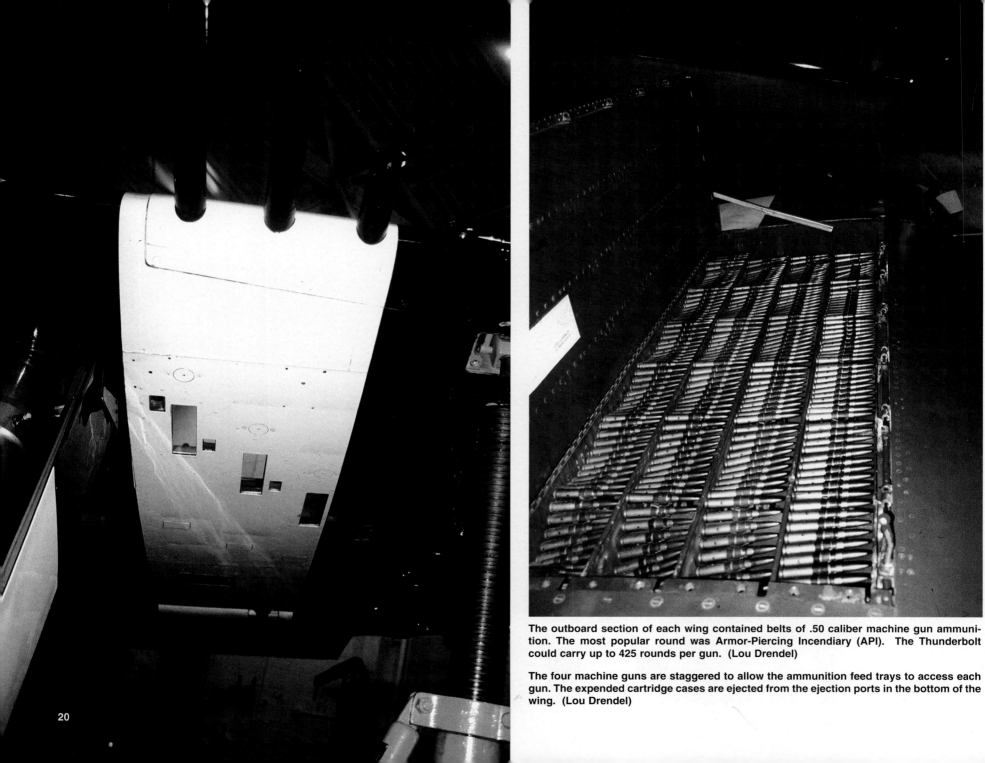

The outboard section of each wing contained belts of .50 caliber machine gun ammunition. The most popular round was Armor-Piercing Incendiary (API). The Thunderbolt could carry up to 425 rounds per gun. (Lou Drendel)

The four machine guns are staggered to allow the ammunition feed trays to access each gun. The expended cartridge cases are ejected from the ejection ports in the bottom of the wing. (Lou Drendel)

The barrels of the eight M-3 .50 caliber machine guns are encased in blast tubes. (Lou Drendel)

A wider view of the open ammunition bay showing the gun numbering system painted on the wing. (Lou Drendel)

The gun camera is located in the starboard wing (small window) adjacent to the cabin air conditioning intake. (Lou Drendel)

(Above) The guns have been removed, but the blast tubes are in place in the gun bay. (Lou Drendel)

Fixed Wing Guns

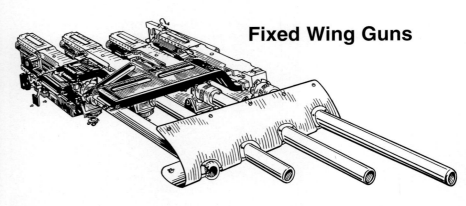

(Below) Four of the eight guns have been removed from this Bradley Field, Connecticut P-47, which was used for fighter training. The gun camera window has also been covered with an add-on fairing. Underwing pylons were added on the -15 variant of the "D" model. Many earlier models were modified to accept these pylons. (Norm Taylor Collection)

P-47Ds of the 121st CCTS-F lined up at Bradley Field, Connecticut. The large crowds on the flight line indicate that an airshow is in progress. (Lt Col Mike Moffitt, USAF (ret) via Norm Taylor Collection)

(Above) Spent cartridge case ejection ports, on the underside of the port wing, looking outboard. (Lou Drendel)

(Right) The wing flaps are not reinforced, so it is critical that they not be used in mounting or dismounting the aircraft. The red paint (common to all P-47 variants) is a reminder to keep off this area. The walkway is painted black and in the flap area is restricted to the small fuselage fairing. The kick-in step is just aft and below this fairing and is not visible in this picture. (Lou Drendel)

(Below) The underside of the port wing, showing the aileron counterweight balances (bumps) and the vortex generating strips on the wing. (Lou Drendel)

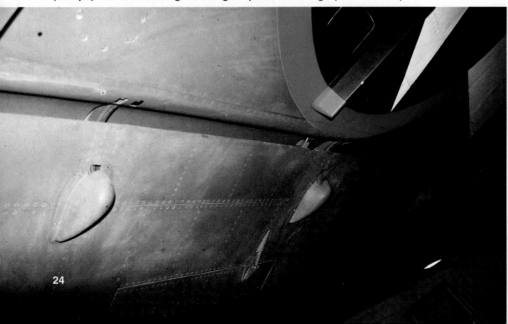

(Above) When the NACA slotted trailing edge flap is fully extended, the hinge cover opens to allow full extension of the flaps. (Lou Drendel)

(Left) An additional view of the underside of the wing, showing the aileron balances and hinge, and the amber position light. (Lou Drendel)

(Below) The retracting landing light is just aft of the main gear well on the port wing. (Lou Drendel)

P-47D-23-RE (42-27828) of the 121st CCTS-F at Bradley Field on 15 August 1944. This was the last of the Razorback versions of the D models. (Lt Col Mike Moffitt, USAF (ret) via Norm Taylor Collection)

Wing Panel Assembly

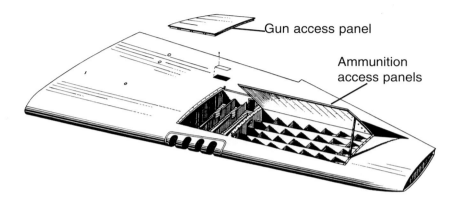

Gun access panel

Ammunition access panels

Underside of port wingtip, showing open inspection panels and position light on the wing tip which is colored bulb enclosed by a clear cover. (Lou Drendel)

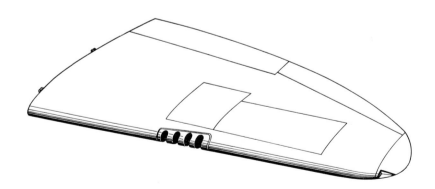

Inspection panels on the bottom of the wing

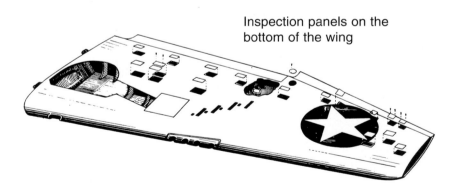

The wing gun blast tubes on "Big Ass Bird II" are as pristine as the rest of this great restoration. (Lou Drendel)

(Right) The underside of left wing, with jack points in use for the annual inspection of the Kalamazoo P-47. (Lou Drendel)

Cockpit air conditioning intake and gun camera access panel on the Kalamazoo P-47. (Lou Drendel)

The flaps in their down postion reveals the mechanism that both lowers and extends them. (Lou Drendel)

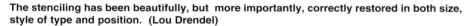

The stenciling has been beautifully, but more importantly, correctly restored in both size, style of type and position. (Lou Drendel)

The .50 caliber link and cartridge ejection chutes run diagonally along the wing just out board of the main landing gear. (Drendel)

The gun camera lens just outboard of the cockpit air conditioning intake on the starboard wing. (Drendel)

(Above) "THE PIED PIPER" was a War Weary veteran of the 318th Fighter Group on Saipan in late 1944. (Pete Bowers via Norm Taylor Collection)

(Below) A P47D of the 121st CCTS.F, cleaned up and rolled out for some publicity pictures. (Norm Taylor Collection)

.50 Caliber Machine Gun

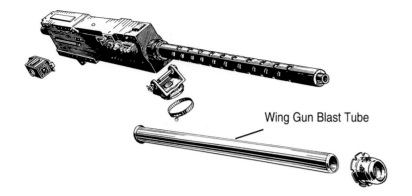

Wing Gun Blast Tube

Built-in Crash Skids

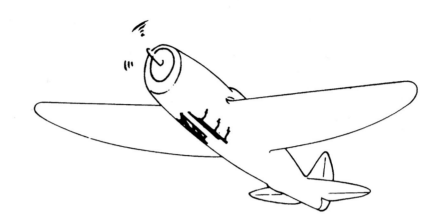

Tail Assembly

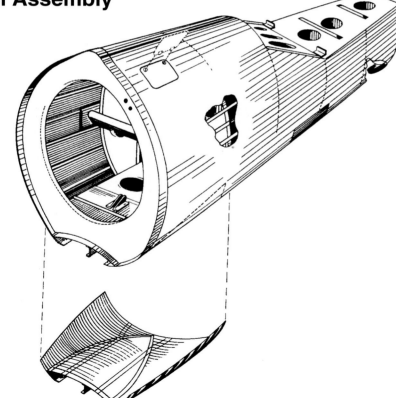

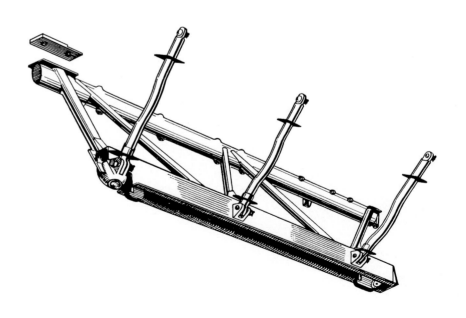

The interior of this open access panel on the under wing seems to be painted Olive Drab rather than the the Interior or Chromate Green that most of the aircraft's interior is painted. (Lou Drendel)

The rear fuselage compartment looking forward. The shelf contains modern avionics. The original equipment carried in this space was radio transmitter and receivers. (Lou Drendel)

The rear fuselage compartment looking aft. The shelf contains an oxygen bottle and avionics. The large duct under the shelf are cooling air ducts for the turbosupercharger. (Lou Drendel)

Details of the aft shelf in the rear fuselage compartment. (Lou Drendel)

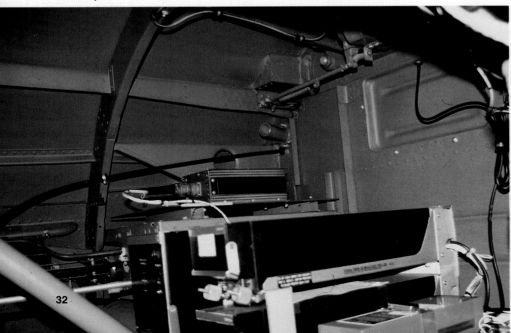

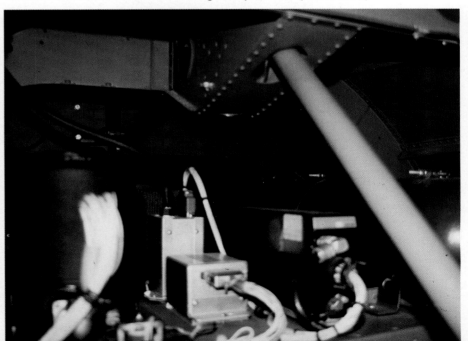

Two of the most complete and authentic civil restorations of the Repulic P-47 Thunderbolt appeared at the annual convention of the Experimental Aircraft Association in Oshkosh, Wisconsin, and the winter extravaganza EAA Sun N' Fun at Lakeland, Florida. "Little Demon" taxies down the Warbird Line at Oshkosh on 29 July 1984. "Big Ass Bird II" basks in the Florida sunshine in April of 1994. (Lou Drendel)

This worn out P-47G-I5-CU was relegated to being a ground instruction vehicle. The candy-striped nose, tail, and wingtips served as warnings, much like the "student driver" signs on instructional autos today. (Peter Bowers via Norm Taylor Collection)

This 318th Fighter Group P-47 made it back to its base on Saipan — but just barely — before being written off on landing. (Wahlberg via Norm Taylor Collection)

603 and 681, a pair of P-47 Thunderbolts from the 346th Fighter Squadron, 350th Fighter Group over Italy in February of 1945. Each aircraft is carrying 165 gallon drop tanks on the wings and 108 gallon drop tanks on the centerline. (Norm Taylor Collection)

P-47D cutway. (Republic via Norm Taylor Collection)

The intercooler exhaust door looking aft. One of the central design features of the Thunderbolt is the fuselage mounted turbosupercharger, which gave the P-47 its outstanding high altitude performance. (Lou Drendel)

(Left) Looking into the starboard side fuselage intercooler exhaust door. (Lou Drendel)

Intercooler exhaust door. Exhaust gases from the engine are ducted along the fuselage sides to the turbine of the supercharger. Ram air for supercharging comes from the air intake below the engine, and is augmented by the propeller. The supercharged air was returned to the engine carburetor via fuselage ducting. The flow of air through the intercooler was controlled by the opening and closing of these doors. (Lou Drendel)

Two civilian restorations of the Thunderbolt, both in the markings of the top scoring Thunderbolt unit in World War II, the 56th Fighter Group.

All the fuselage access panels have been opened on the Kalamazoo P-47 for its annual inspection. (Lou Drendel)

Rudder hinge cover on the starboard side. (Lou Drendel)

The open underwing access panels, looking inboard on the port wing. (Lou Drendel)

Armament

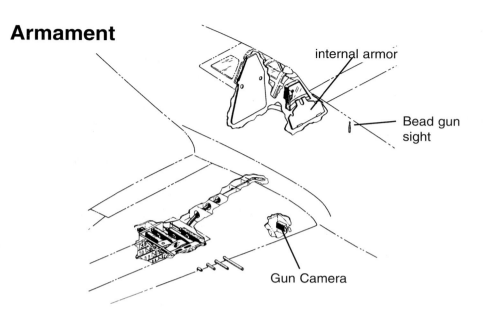

internal armor

Bead gun sight

Gun Camera

(Left) The antenna just above the open fuselage access panel is for modern avionics. (Lou Drendel)

A P-47D-28-RA (42-29002) of the 64th Fighter Squadron, 57th Fighter Group operating in the Mediterranean Theater of Operations (MTO) in 1944 and 1945. (Roger Besecker via Norm Taylor Collection)

The turbosupercharger exhaust fairing under the fuselage. Exhaust gases are discharged here after passing through the supercharger turbine. (Lou Drendel)

The intercooler exhaust doors, on the port side of the fuselage. (Lou Drendel)

Access panels on the starboard side of the fuselage indicate locations of supercharger oil, data case, and oxygen. (Lou Drendel)

Though it is painted to represent the P-47 flown by Howard Park of the 513th FS, 406th FG of the 9th AF, "Big Ass Bird II" is actually a P-47D-40 (44-90368), built in Evansville, Indiana and accepted by the Army Air Forces on 7 May 1945. The Venezuela Air Force acquired it on 28 August 1947. It remained in Venezuela for 40 years before being sold to a French warbird collector, who in turn sold it to Charles Osborn. (Lou Drendel)

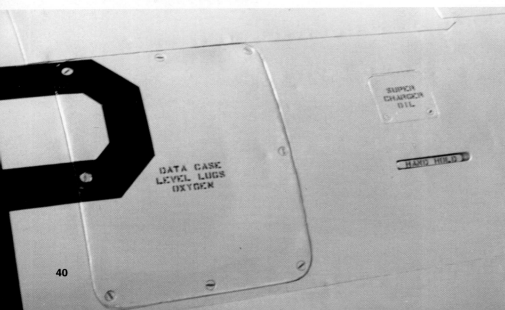

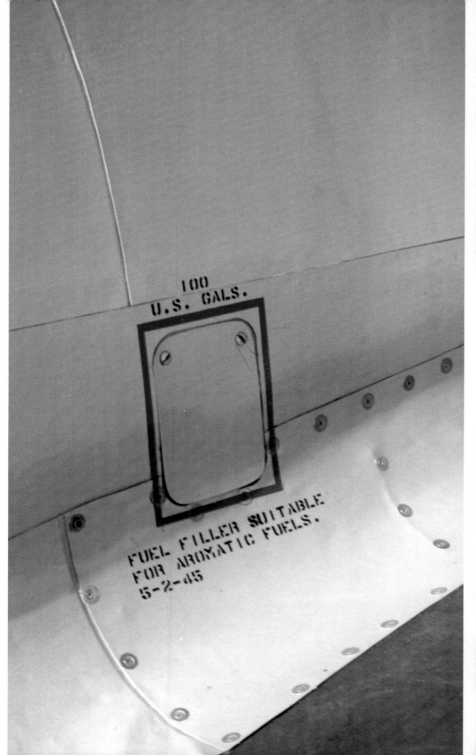

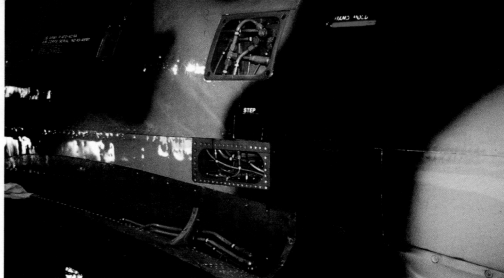

(Above) Open fuselage access panels show some of the fuel, hydraulic and electrical lines. (Lou Drendel)

(Left) Much of the room in the fuselage is taken up by the turbosupercharger components, and the wings are filled with landing gear and machine guns, so internal fuel in the P-47 is limited to a 205 gallon fuel tank in front of the cockpit, and a 100 gallon tank under the pilot's seat. The access panel for the latter is on the right side of the fuselage. Internal fuel capacity was upped to 370 gallons in the D-25 model. (Lou Drendel)

(Below) The flaps are in the full-down position. (Lou Drendel)

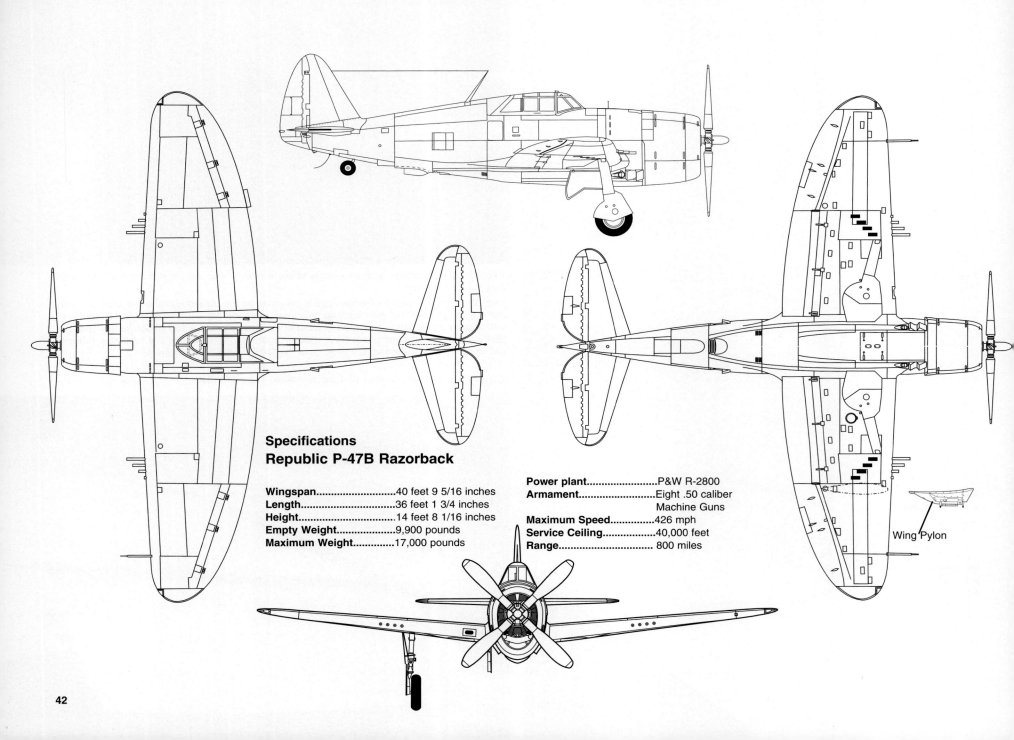

Specifications
Republic P-47B Razorback

Wingspan...........................40 feet 9 5/16 inches
Length................................36 feet 1 3/4 inches
Height................................14 feet 8 1/16 inches
Empty Weight...................9,900 pounds
Maximum Weight..............17,000 pounds

Power plant........................P&W R-2800
Armament...........................Eight .50 caliber
                                        Machine Guns
Maximum Speed...............426 mph
Service Ceiling.................40,000 feet
Range................................ 800 miles

Wing Pylon

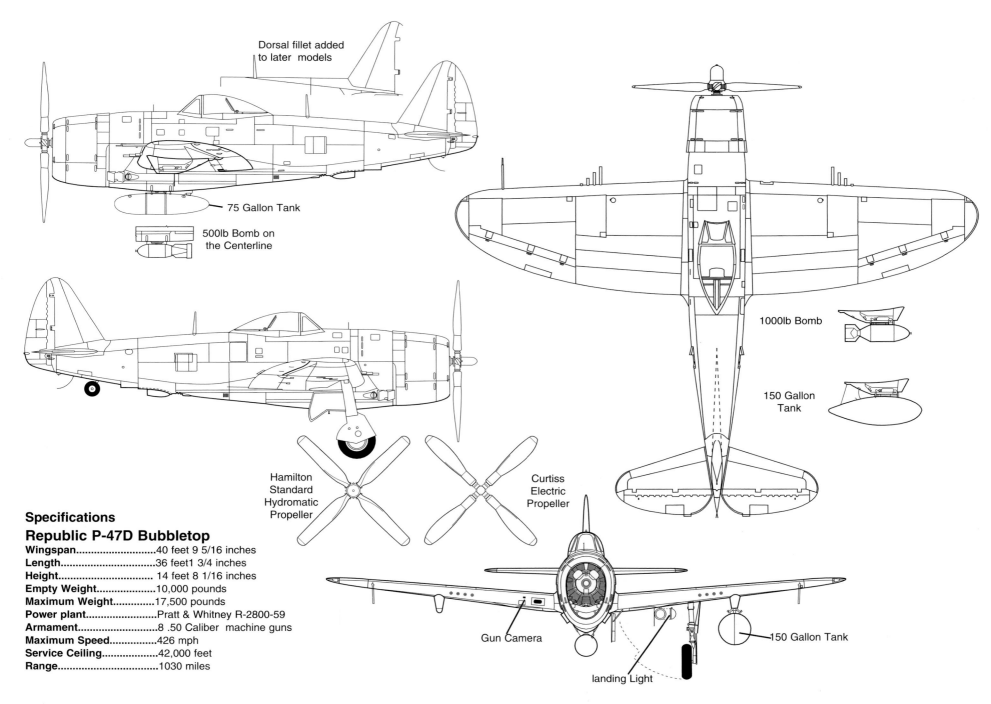

Dorsal fillet added
to later models

75 Gallon Tank

500lb Bomb on
the Centerline

1000lb Bomb

150 Gallon
Tank

Hamilton
Standard
Hydromatic
Propeller

Curtiss
Electric
Propeller

Gun Camera

landing Light

150 Gallon Tank

Specifications
Republic P-47D Bubbletop

Wingspan...........................40 feet 9 5/16 inches
Length................................36 feet1 3/4 inches
Height................................ 14 feet 8 1/16 inches
Empty Weight....................10,000 pounds
Maximum Weight..............17,500 pounds
Power plant........................Pratt & Whitney R-2800-59
Armament...........................8 .50 Caliber machine guns
Maximum Speed................426 mph
Service Ceiling..................42,000 feet
Range..................................1030 miles

SUPERCHARGER OIL TANK
1.5 U.S. GALS. GRADE 1065

HAND HOLD

Flap markings indicate degrees of flap deployed, used in lieu of a cockpit gauge. (Lou Drendel)

Supercharger oil tank access door and retractable hand hold on the starboard side of fuselage. (Lou Drendel)

Top of port wing, showing the access panel to the transfer valve. (Lou Drendel)

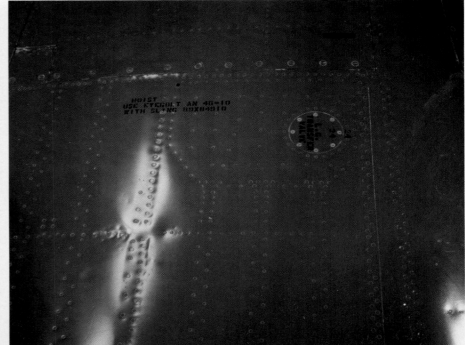

(Above) War emergency power of 2,300 HP is available with water methanol injection in the Pratt & Whitney R-2800. (Lou Drendel)

(Left)The P-47 is powered by the Pratt & Whitney R-2800 Double Wasp 18 cylinder two-row air-cooled radial engine with a General Electric turbosupercharger, rated at 2,000 HP for takeoff at sea level, and military power at 27,000 feet. (Lou Drendel)

(Below) The ground electric plug is behind and below the access panel and above the oil cooler exhaust variable shutter and fixed deflector. (Lou Drendel)

Maintenance being pulled by mechanics of the 86th Fighter Group. (Merle Olmsted via Norm Taylor Collection)

(Left) The P-47 Thunderbolt was the first U.S. fighter to use a four blade propeller. It took a 12 foot diameter propellor to handle the power generated by the R-2800 engine. The original propeller was a Curtiss Electric C542S-A-6 of 12 foot 2 inch diameter. (Norm Taylor Collection)

Mechanics of the 527th Fighter Squadron preparing to install a new engine in a Thunderbolt at Munich, Germany in 1949. (Merle Olmsted via Norm Taylor Collection)

Boresighting the guns of a 527th FS, 86th FG, USAF F-47 at Neubiburg AB, Germany in 1948. Although it was the jet age, many fighter squadrons continued to fly the best World War II fighters on active duty. (Merle Olmsted via Norm Taylor Collection)

An uncowled oil cooler exhaust shutter on the starboard side. (Lou Drendel)

(Left) The reduction gear is contained within the large casing behind the propeller. Magnetos are on the top of this casing, one on either side of the propeller governor. (Lou Drendel)

The intake for the turbosupercharger intercooler is in the center, while the oil cooler intakes are on either side of the lower engine bay. (Lou Drendel)

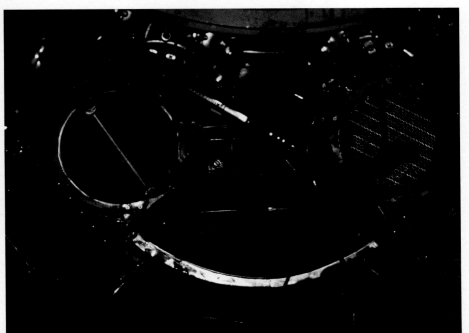

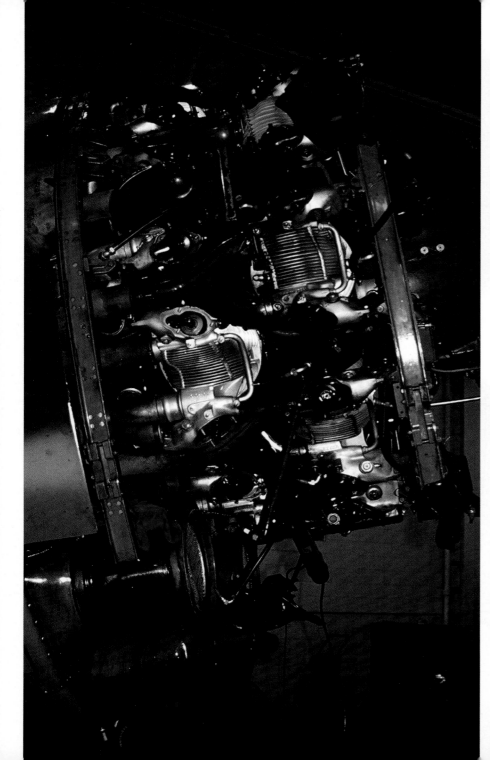

A 28 volt electrical plug allows for starting from ground start-carts when necessary. This plug is normally covered by an access panel. (Lou Drendel)

(Left) The port side of an uncowled R-2800 engine. (Lou Drendel)

The 28.6 gallon oil tank; it took a lot of oil to lubricate the big R-2800 engine. (Lou Drendel)

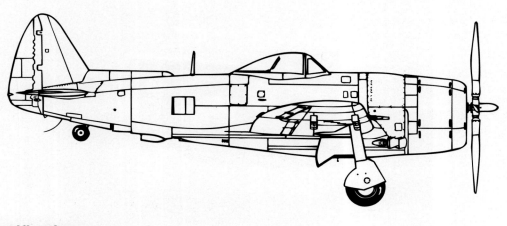

Specifications
Republic P-47N-1-RE

Wingspan............................42 feet 7 inches
Length................................36 feet 1 inch
Height.................................14 feet 8 inches
Empty Weight...................10,988 pounds
Loaded Weight..................21,200 pounds

Power plant...One R-2800 hp Pratt & Whitney
                                                         18 cylinder air cooled engine
Armament.. Six or eight .50 caliber Machine guns
Maximum Speed............................. 467 mph
Service Ceiling................................ 43,000 feet
Max Range...2,000 miles

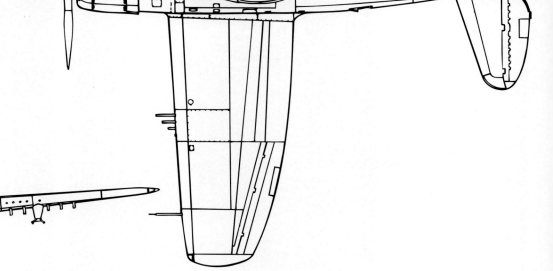

Invasion Stripes

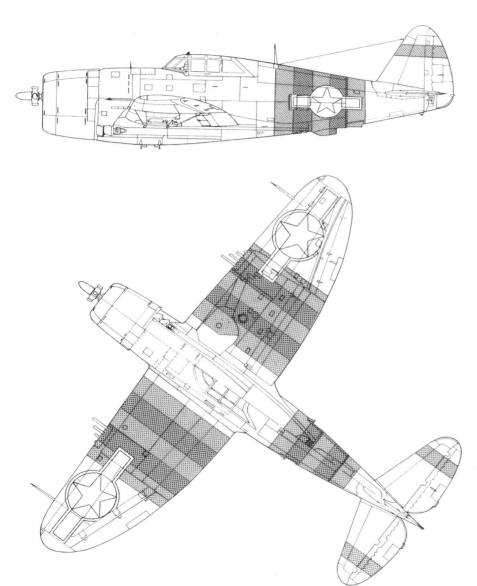

(Above) "Zombie" a natural metal Thunderbolt of the 78th Fighter Group is carrying full D-Day Invasion Stripes. (AFM via Davis)

(Below) With a heavily damaged port wing, the 367th Fighter Squadron pilot brought this P-47D-20 home. Black and White Invasion Stripes have been applied to both upper and lower wing surfaces as well as on the fuselage. (Olmsted via Davis)

A checkered Thunderbolt of the 83rd Fighter Squadron, 78th Fighter Group. Easy removal of the cowl and accessory bay panels quickly opened up the engine and accessories to complete maintenance. (The Betty Stadt Collection)

Re-arming the Thunderbolt's wing mounted .50 caliber machine guns was a task that could be completed easily and quickly by the armorers. The eight .50 caliber machine guns could pump out 773 lbs of lead per minute making the P-47 the most potent ground attack aircraft in the Allied arsenal. (The Betty Stadt Collection)

Portions of the exhaust collector rings are visible behind the cowl flaps. The large red colored box contains the 24 volt battery. (Lou Drendel)

Exhaust Manifold

Engine Mount Assembly

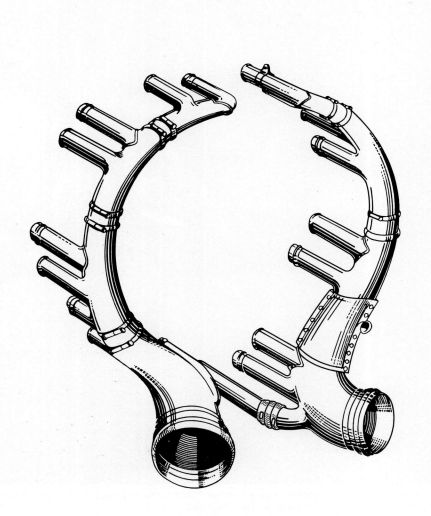

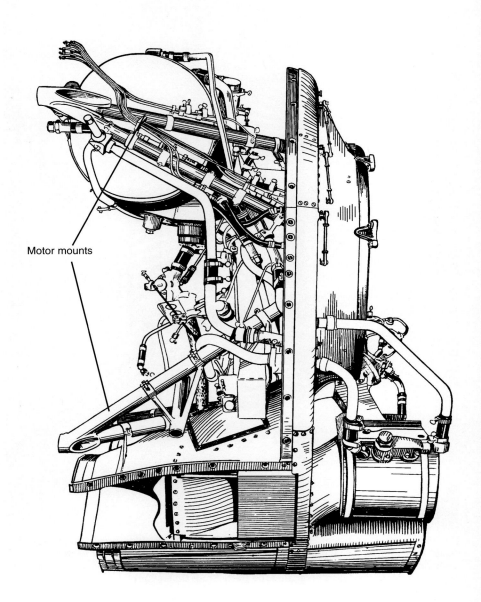

Motor mounts

Engine, Engine Mounts, Accessory Compartment

Hydraulic Units

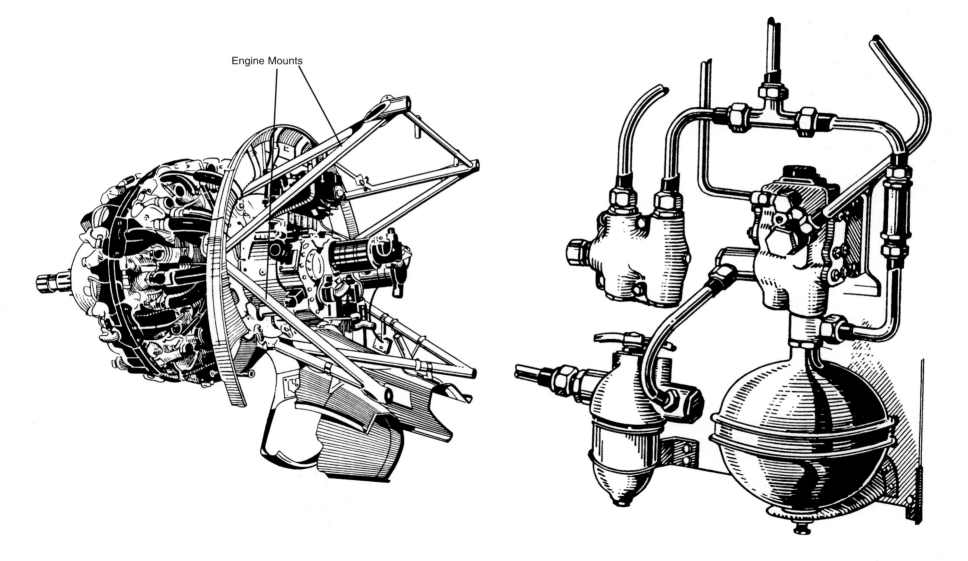

Engine Mounts

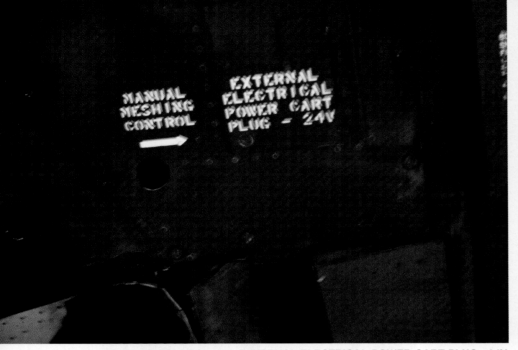

MANUAL MESHING CONTROL and EXTERNAL ELECTRICAL POWER CART PLUG - 24V indicate two methods of starting a P-47 from outside the cockpit. (Lou Drendel)

The Kalamazoo Air Museum P-47 undergoing its annual inspection. The large access panel open on the fuselage reveals part of the extensive ducting for the turbosupercharger. (Lou Drendel)

The underside of the propeller reduction casing, with oil lines visible. (Lou Drendel)

Inside and outside views of the starboard main landing gear. The combination of the big, 12 foot diameter propeller, which required long landing legs, and limited space in the wing for retraction, led to development of a telescoping landing gear leg, which shortened by nine inches during retraction. (Lou Drendel)

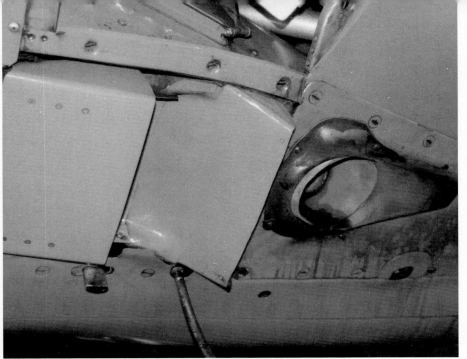

(Above) The port side engine exhaust. (Lou Drendel)

(Left) Port side of the accessory compartment just behind the engine. (Lou Drendel)

(Below) Prop spinner hub and cuffs from behind. (Lou Drendel)

(Below) The actual full diameter of the Curtiss Electric propeller is 12 feet 2 inches. (Lou Drendel)

(Above and below) Engine cowlings removed from an F-47D-30-RA of the 86th Fighter Group in Germany during 1949. A number of access panels are open as this occupation force Thunderbolt undergoes a major maintenance event. Also worthy of note is the fact that the guns have been removed. This was a forward operating location, with PSP ramps. (Merle Olmsted via Norm Taylor)

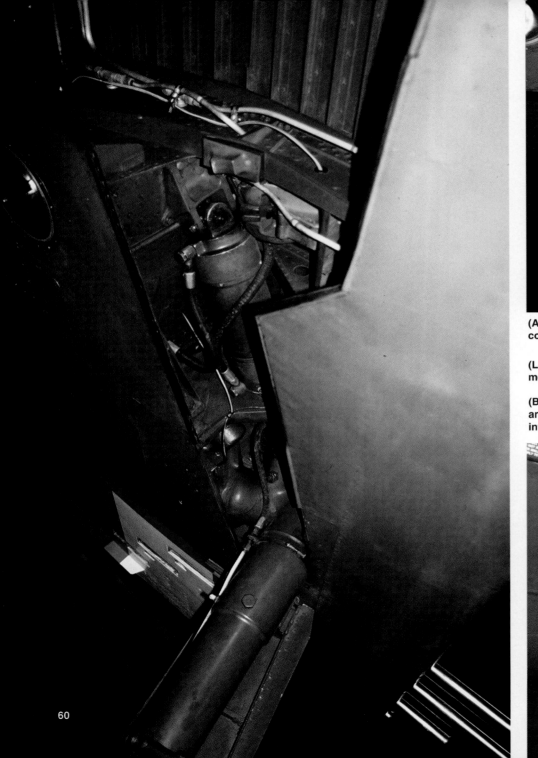

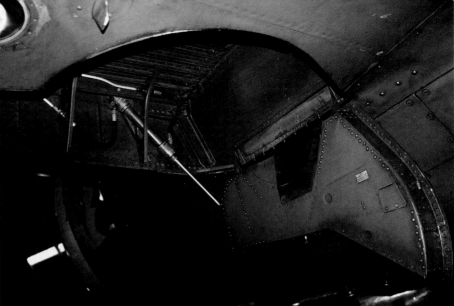

(Above) The actuating arm on the inboard wheel well cover is attached to the front of the cover. (Lou Drendel)

(Left) The port main gear well looking outboard. The various hydraulic lines are natural metal. (Lou Drendel)

(Below) The port main gear well and inboard door. The slight indentation on both the door and the well wall was to accomodate the retracted wheel, indicating the close tolerances involved in full gear retraction. (Lou Drendel)

(Above) The unpainted metal plate on top of the inboard gear door is not a patch, but is part of the door construction. (Lou Drendel)

(Right and Below) The starboard main gear well, looking outboard provides a good view of the hydraulic retraction cylinder. The hydraulic lines on the lower wheel well have been oversprayed with Chromate Green which would easily happen during a repair, while the lines at right are in an unblemished state. (Lou Drendel)

(Above) This battle-damaged P47D-30-RA (44-33050) of the 324th Fighter Group is at Haguenau, France in September of 1944. The Jug was one of the most rugged allied fighters, which meant that it carried the brunt of the air-to-ground attack in the tactical air war in Europe. (Chris Gooman via Norm Taylor Collection)

(Below) A P-47D-28-RA of the 35th fighter Group on Luzon in 1945. (Pete Bowers via Norm Taylor Collection)

Main Landing Gear

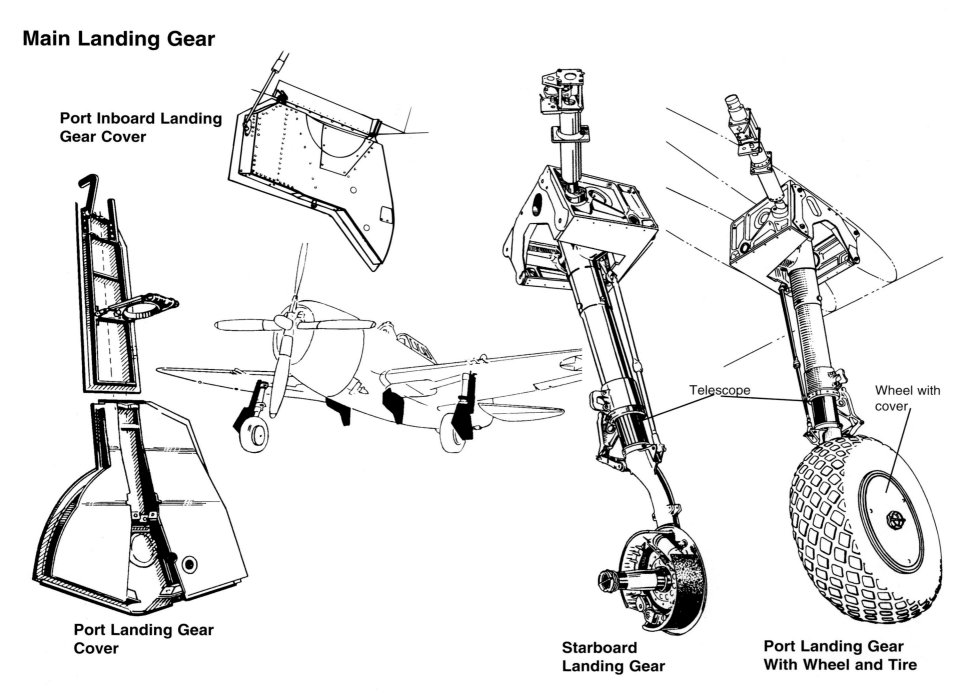

Port Inboard Landing Gear Cover

Port Landing Gear Cover

Telescope

Wheel with cover

Starboard Landing Gear

Port Landing Gear With Wheel and Tire

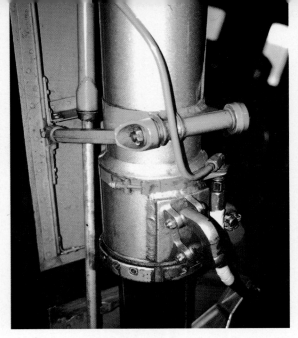

The long rod at left telescopes the main gear leg nine inches, allowing retraction into a gear well which would not otherwise accomodate the long main landing gear legs of the P-47. (Lou Drendel)

The main gear scissors. The uplock U-flange is at the upper right. (Lou Drendel)

The main gear wheel without wheel cover. (Lou Drendel)

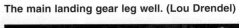

The main landing gear leg well. (Lou Drendel)

Another view of the main gear well, with a clearer picture of the indentation which accomodates the tire when retracted. (Lou Drendel)

Main gear leg details just above the scissors. (Lou Drendel)

The retractable tail wheel was free castering when unlocked. It went to the locked position automatically when the main gear was lowered. (Lou Drendel)

(Right) The inside of the tail wheel doors were painted Chromate Green. (Lou Drendel)

Different batches of Chromate Green could and did vary considerably in color, ranging from an Apple Green to an almost Olive Drab. (Lou Drendel)

Tail Wheel

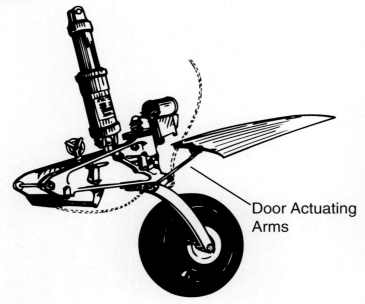

Door Actuating Arms

Tail Wheel Doors

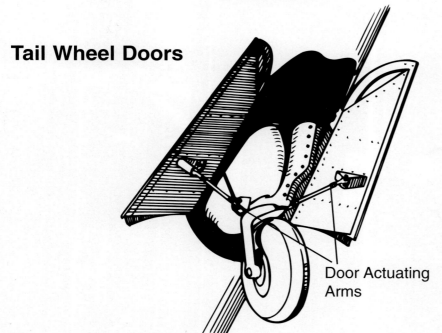

Door Actuating Arms

Stencils on the Neutral Gray tail wheel doors are in white. (Lou Drendel)

A P-47D-30-RE (44-33071) of the 397th Fighter Squadron, 368th Fighter Group in Germany during 1945. The squadron color of the 397th was Blue. (Norm Taylor Collection)

Lt Col S.T. Smith, Jr. of the 80th Fighter Squadron in Burma. (Norm Taylor Collection)

P-47D "Swamp Baby" and pilot Mitchel of the 355th Fighter Squadron. (Norm Taylor Collection)

A P-47D-22-RE of the 360th FS, 356th FG. The A-2 leather jacket, fifty mission crush cap, and upturned bill on the crew chief's cap are all vintage World War Two icons. (Norm Taylor Collection)

Col. Francis "Gabby" Gabreski, one of the top scoring allied aces in WWII was at Lackland AFB, Texas for dedication of their P-47 display, which was painted in the markings of Gabreski's 56th Fighter Group Thunderbolt. (Norm Taylor Collection)

(Above) The electrical panel is just forward and below the throttle quadrant. (Lou Drendel)

(Left) The throttle quadrant of the P-47D. The red knob controls the fuel mixture, the large lever is the throttle (controls manifold pressure) and the small black lever controls the propeller (RPM). The small knob outboard controls the supercharger. At high altitudes, pushing the throttle all the way forward automatically increased prop RPM and the supercharger was full forward. (Lou Drendel)

(Below) Wide view of the port side of the P-47 cockpit. The knobs behind the landing gear control are trim-tab controls. (Lou Drendel)

The starboard side of the P-47 cockpit. The Black box with digital windows contains modern avionics. (Lou Drendel)

(Right) Overhead view of the port side of the cockpit. The round projection at top is an ash tray.

The port side of the cockpit, showing landing gear handle and flap control handle. (Lou Drendel)

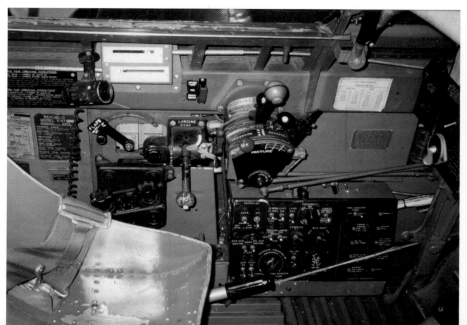

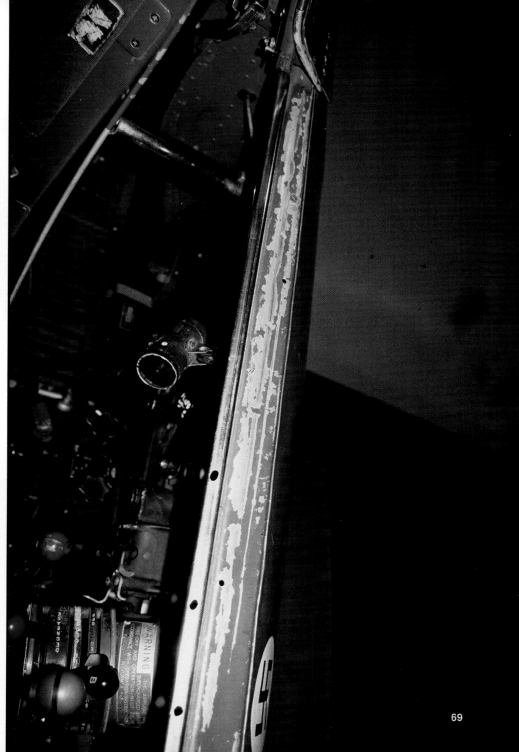

The cockpit armor plate has been removed from the Lone Star P-47, and a rear seat added. (Lou Drendel)

(Left) Although the layout of the Lone Star P-47 cockpit is generally correct from a historical standpoint, for reasons of flight safety a number of modern instruments have been added. These include engine monitoring instruments and several avionics. The boxes on the lower right side of the instrument panel contain modern avionics. The instrument at lower left of the instrument panel is a Glide Slope/Localizer receiver. (Lou Drendel)

Armored Glass

Cockpit

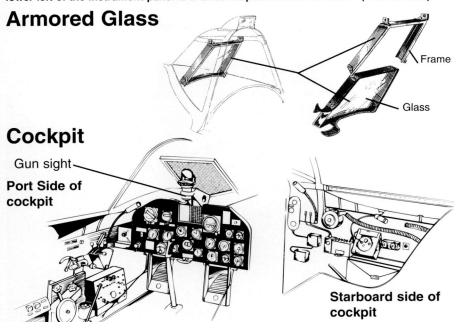

Cockpit Cases

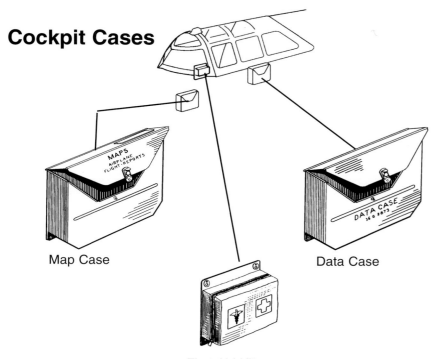

Map Case

Data Case

First Aid Kit

Seat

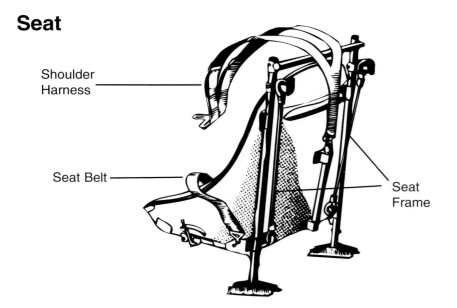

Shoulder
Harness

Seat Belt

Seat
Frame

Windshield/Canopy

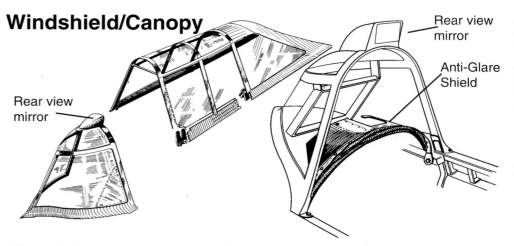

Rear view
mirror

Rear view
mirror

Anti-Glare
Shield

The gunsights are authentic in the Lone Star P-47, and include the simple ring and post sight as well as a reflector gunsight. The reflector gunsight is comprised of a light, a reticle, a lens, and a transparent mirror. The light illuminates the reticle, which is placed at focal length from the lens. The image formed is reflected to the eye by the transparent mirror which is just a piece of glass whose sides are perfectly flat and parallel. Since it is a transparent mirror, the image appears to originate at infinity. (Lou Drendel)

The box on extreme right side contains modern avionics. (Lou Drendel)

Bubble canopy of P-47D, showing the back of the armor plate, and canopy track details.

The Control stick with a well-worn leather and canvas boot covering the cable connections at its base. The small red knob in front of the boot is the control lock, which enables the pilot to lock all controls when the aircraft is parked, preventing damage from wind gusts. (Lou Drendel)

The seat in the P-47 was made to accomodate a seat pack parachute. The seat was adjustable for height only. Short legs were accomodated by adjusting the rudder pedals in or out. The additional lever at the extreme left of the picture is the tail wheel lock to help you maintain directional control when 2,000 horses and a 12 foot prop were trying to turn a hard left! (Lou Drendel)

The P-47D armor plate and seat top. The Blue cushion is strictly civilian. The armor plate was advertised to be able to stop direct right angle hits by all .30 caliber rounds, including U.S., German, Japanese, and Italian. (Lou Drendel)

All photos on this page are P-47Ns of the 19th Fighter Squadron, 318th Fighter Group, on Ie Shima in 1945. Ie Shima is an island three miles off the coast of Okinawa, and 325 miles from Japan. The P-47Ns of the 318th flew the 4,100 miles from Hawaii to Ie Shima in stages. All P-47Ns that saw action in the Pacific were built at Republic's Farmingdale plant, with production beginning in December of 1944. Of note: Tropical flying uniforms consisted of khaki shirt and pants, Mae West, pistol belt and an M-1911 Colt .45 pistol. (Norm Taylor Collection)

"The Repulsive Thunderbox", a P-47N-1 -RE (44-88119) one of the 550 N-1s built. The principle differences between the N and D models included the addition of 200 gallons of internal fuel in tanks added in the wing root area, adding 24 inches to the landing gear track. The square-cut wing tips added 18 inches of wing span. (Pete Bowers collection via Norm Taylor Collection)

P-47N of the 507th Fighter Group, which arrived on Ie Shima in June of 1945. The principle duty of the 507th was fighter escort for B-29s bombing the Japanese homeland. However, the reputation of the Thunderbolt as a rugged ground attacker resulted in a mission adjustment, hence the bombing mission markers under the cockpit. (Norm Taylor Collection)

P-47Ns bound for Hawaii on the deck of a carrier. They would be lifted off and subsequently flown to Ie Shima by the 318th FG. The N model was designed for long range missions, and was equipped with an autopilot to ease pilot fatigue. (Norm Taylor Collection)

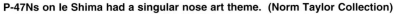

P-47Ns on Ie Shima had a singular nose art theme. (Norm Taylor Collection)

An F-47N-25-RE (44-89347) of the 101st Fighter Squadron, Massachussetts ANG at Logan Airport on 17 November 1949. (Paul Paulsen via Norm Taylor Collection)

P-47N-20-RA, one of 149 built in Evansville, next to a war-weary D model at Marietta AFB, Georgia in December of 1946. Also worthy of note is the addition of a red stripe on the wing national insignia. (Norm Taylor Collection)

An F-47N-25-RE (44-89404) of the 142nd Fighter Squadron of the Delaware ANG at New Castle, Delaware in 1950. The 142nd flew Thunderbolts from 1946 to 1950. (Roger Besecker via Norm Taylor Collection)

A P-47D-40-RE (45-49431). At the end of World War II there were over 3,000 Thunderbolts in Europe and 1,400 in the Pacific. Many were shipped back to the United States, hundreds were broken up for scrap, and many more were given to allied nations, either to supplement their air forces or to build a new air force. (Roger Besecker collection via Norm Taylor Collection)

A P-47N-5-RE (44-88651) The P-47N weighed over 1,000 more pounds empty than the D model, and grossed 20,700 lbs fully loaded, the highest takeoff weight for any single-engine fighter to that time. (Roger Besecker via Norm Taylor Collection)

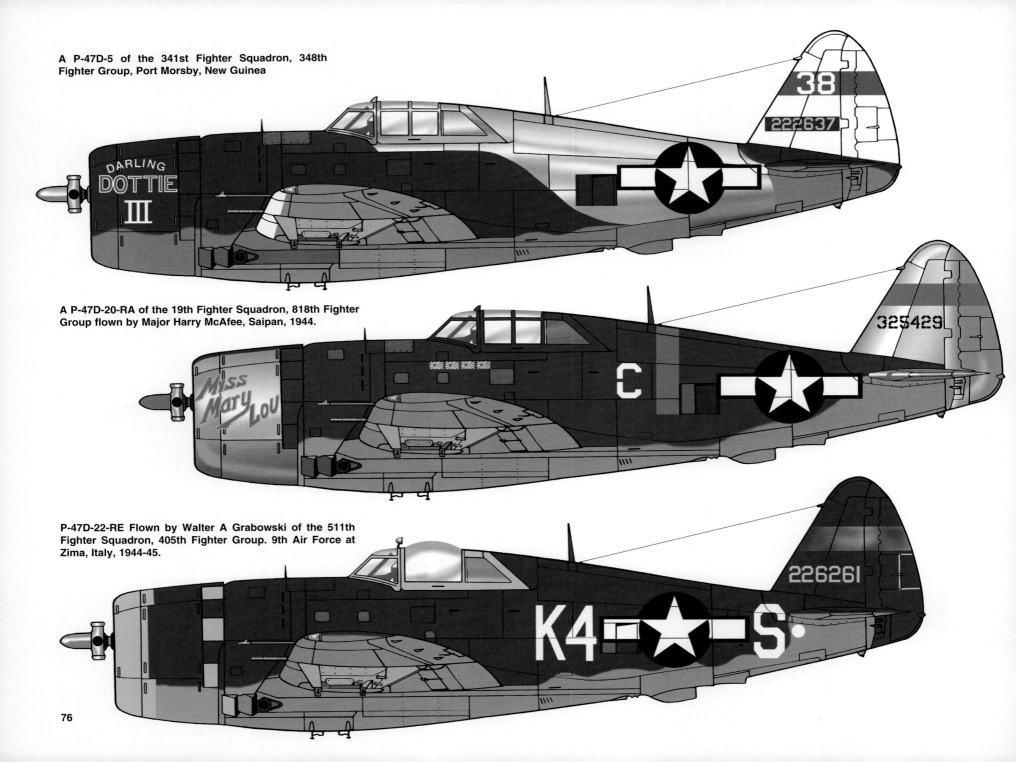

A P-47D-5 of the 341st Fighter Squadron, 348th Fighter Group, Port Morsby, New Guinea

A P-47D-20-RA of the 19th Fighter Squadron, 818th Fighter Group flown by Major Harry McAfee, Saipan, 1944.

P-47D-22-RE Flown by Walter A Grabowski of the 511th Fighter Squadron, 405th Fighter Group. 9th Air Force at Zima, Italy, 1944-45.

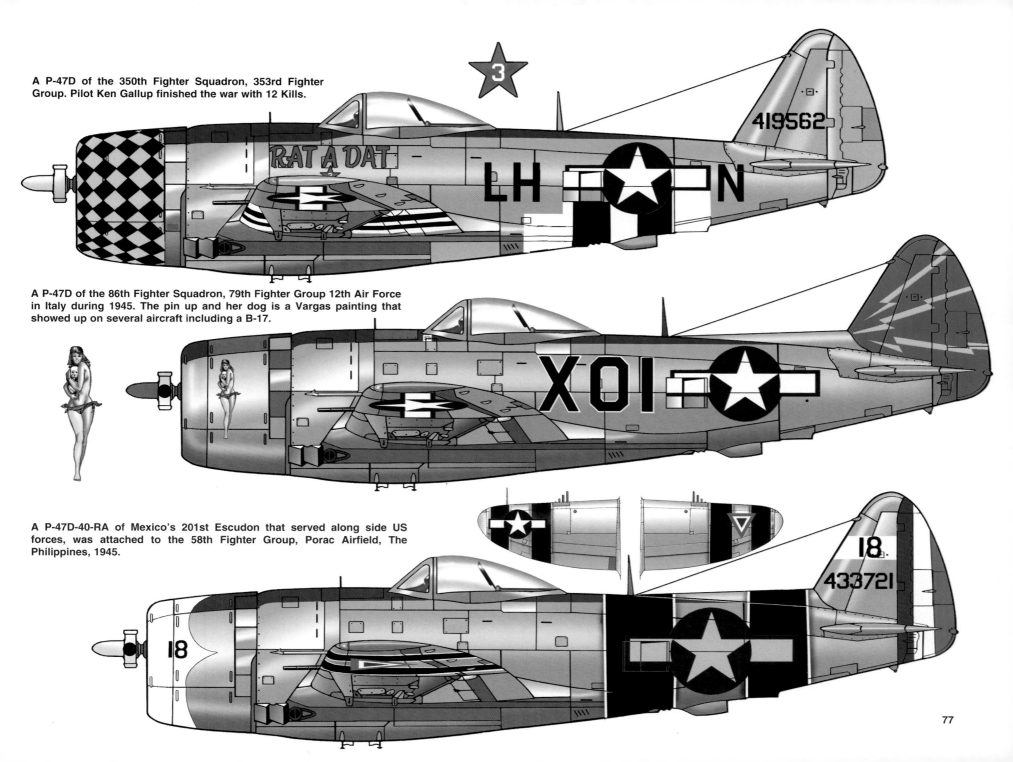

A P-47D of the 350th Fighter Squadron, 353rd Fighter Group. Pilot Ken Gallup finished the war with 12 Kills.

A P-47D of the 86th Fighter Squadron, 79th Fighter Group 12th Air Force in Italy during 1945. The pin up and her dog is a Vargas painting that showed up on several aircraft including a B-17.

A P-47D-40-RA of Mexico's 201st Escudon that served along side US forces, was attached to the 58th Fighter Group, Porac Airfield, The Philippines, 1945.

F-47Ds of the 104th Fighter Squadron of the Maryland Air National Guard. The Thunderbolt was operated by 24 different state ANG units between 1946 and 1955. (Norm Taylor Collection)

F-47D of the 86th Fighter Group was modified with Russian markings for its part in the movie "*Berlin Airlift*" in 1949. The 86th was the last unit to operate the Thunderbolt in Europe. (Merle Olmsted via Norm Taylor Collection)

A Crew chief doing an engine run up on an F-47D of the 86th Fighter Group at Neubiburg, Germany in 1948. (Merle Olmsted via Norm Taylor Collection)

F-47D-30-RA (44-33215) came to grief in a landing accident. Destruction of the masonry wall demonstrates the rugged nature of the Jug. (Norm Taylor Collection)

A non-standard P-38 drop tank fitted to a TP47D-40-RA (45-49344). It carries zero length rocket launch rails under the wing, however, the guns have been removed. The D-40 was the last of the D models with 665 built in Evansville. (Roger Besecker via Norm Taylor Collection)

(Below) A P47D-30-RA (44-90021). The D-30-RA was the most heavily produced variant, with 1,800 rolling off the Evansville production line. (Roger Besecker collection via Norm Taylor Collection)

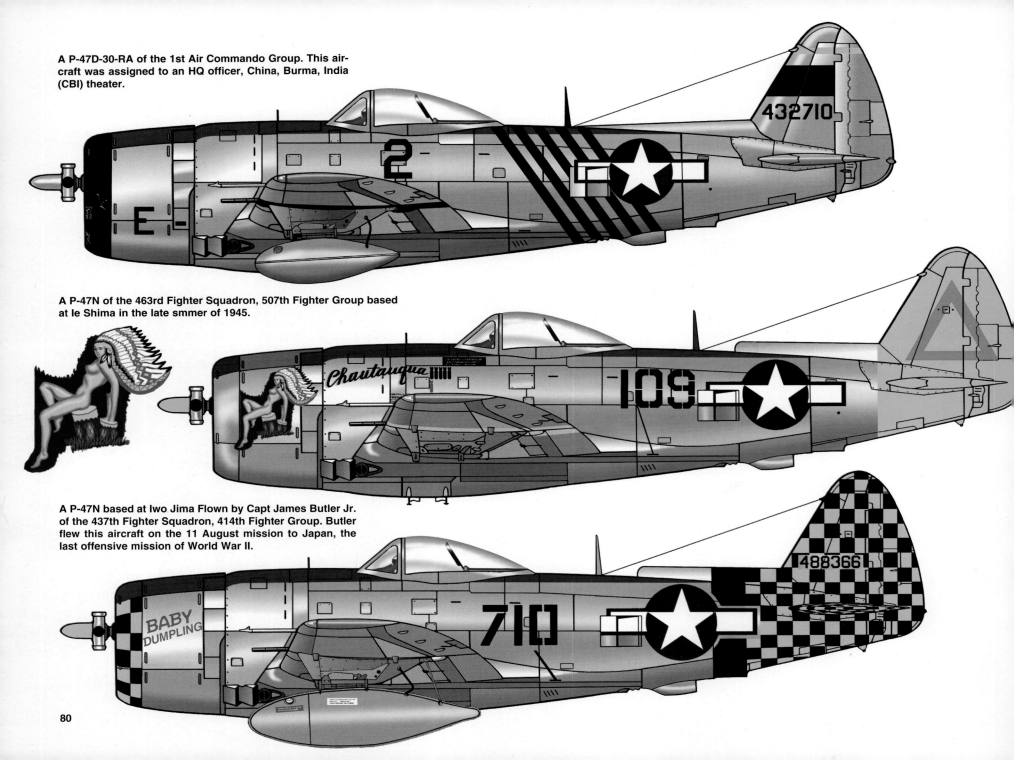

A P-47D-30-RA of the 1st Air Commando Group. This aircraft was assigned to an HQ officer, China, Burma, India (CBI) theater.

A P-47N of the 463rd Fighter Squadron, 507th Fighter Group based at Ie Shima in the late smmer of 1945.

A P-47N based at Iwo Jima Flown by Capt James Butler Jr. of the 437th Fighter Squadron, 414th Fighter Group. Butler flew this aircraft on the 11 August mission to Japan, the last offensive mission of World War II.